Indian Frontier Policy

JOHN ADYE

1897

TABLE OF CONTENTS

PREFACE

The subject of our policy on the North-West frontier of India is one of great importance, as affecting the general welfare of our Eastern Empire, and is specially interesting at the present time, when military operations on a considerable scale are being conducted against a combination of the independent tribes along the frontier.

It must be understood that the present condition of affairs is no mere sudden outbreak on the part of our turbulent neighbours. Its causes lie far deeper, and are the consequences of events in bygone years.

In the following pages I have attempted to give a short historical summary of its varying phases, in the hope that I may thus assist the public in some degree to understand its general bearings, and to form a correct opinion of the policy which should be pursued in the future.

JOHN ADYE,
General.

EVENTS PRIOR TO, AND INCLUDING, FIRST AFGHAN WAR OF 1839-41

In considering the important and somewhat intricate subject of policy on the North-Western frontier of our Indian Empire it will be desirable, in the first place, to give a concise history of the events which have guided our action, and which for many years past have exercised a predominating influence in that part of our Eastern dominion.

Speaking generally, it may, I think, be said that the main features of our policy on the North-Western frontier have been determined by the gradual advance of Russia southwards, and partly also by the turbulent character of the people of Afghanistan, and of the independent tribes who inhabit the great region of mountains which lie between Russia and ourselves.

These two circumstances—the first having been the most powerful—have led us into great wars and frontier expeditions, which as a rule have been costly, and in some cases unjust, and their consequences have not tended to strengthen our position either on the frontier or in India itself.

It will be well therefore to give an outline of the Russian conquests in Central Asia to the north of Afghanistan, and also of our dealings with the rulers of Cabul in bygone years, and we shall then be better able to judge of our present position, and to determine the principles which should guide our North-Western frontier policy.

One of the first threats of invasion of India early in the century was planned at Tilsit, and is thus described by Kaye:

[Footnote: History of the War in Afghanistan] 'Whilst the followers of Alexander and Napoleon were abandoning themselves to convivial pleasures, those monarchs were spending quiet evenings together discussing their future plans, and projecting joint schemes of conquest. It was then that they meditated the invasion of Hindostan by a confederate army uniting on the plains of Persia; and no secret was made of the intention of the two great European potentates to commence in the following spring a hostile demonstration—Contre les possessions de la compagnie des Indes.'

The peril, however, was averted by a treaty at Teheran in March 1809, in which the Shah of Persia covenanted not to permit any European force whatever to pass through Persia towards India, or towards the ports of that country. And so the visionary danger passed away.

The old southern boundary of Russia in Central Asia extended from the north of the Caspian by Orenburg and Orsk, across to the old Mongolian city of Semipalatinsk, and was guarded by a cordon of forts and Cossack outposts. It was about 2,000 miles in length, and [Footnote: Quarterly Review, Oct. 1865.] 'abutted on the great Kirghis Steppe, and to a certain extent controlled the tribes pasturing in the vicinity, but by no means established the hold of Russia on that pathless, and for the most part lifeless, waste.'

During all the earlier years of the century, while we were establishing our power in India, constant intrigues and wars occurred in Persia, Afghanistan, and Central Asia; and rumours were occasionally heard of threats against ourselves, which formed the subject of diplomatic treatment from time to time; but in reality the scene was so distant that our interests were not seriously affected, and it was not until 1836 that they began to exercise a powerful influence as regards our policy on the North-West frontier.

In that year Lord Auckland was Governor-General, and Captain Alexander Burnes was sent on a commercial mission up the Indus, and through the Kyber Pass, to Cabul, where he was received in a friendly manner by the Ameer Dost Mahomed. It must be borne in mind that neither Scinde nor the Punjaub was then under our rule, so that our frontiers were still far distant from Afghanistan. It was supposed at the time that Russia was advancing southward towards India in league with Persia, and the mission of Burnes was in reality political, its object being to induce the Ameer to enter into a friendly alliance.

Dost Mahomed was quite willing to meet our views, and offered to give up altogether any connection with the two Powers named. It, however, soon became apparent that our interests were by no means identical; his great object, as we found, being to recover the Peshawur district, which had been taken a few years previously by Runjeet Singh, while we, on the other hand, courted his friendship chiefly in order that his country might prove a barrier against the advance of Russia and Persia.

These respective views were evidently divergent and the issues doubtful; when suddenly a Russian Envoy (Vicovitch), also on a so-called commercial mission, arrived at Cabul, offering the Ameer money and assistance against the Sikhs. This altered the aspect of affairs. Burnes wrote to the Governor-General that the Russians were evidently trying to outbid us. Still some hope remained, until definite instructions arrived from Lord Auckland declining to mediate with or to act against Runjeet Singh, the ruler of the Punjaub. The Ameer felt that we made great demands on him but gave him nothing in return. It then became evident that the mission of Burnes was a failure, and in April 1838 he returned to India. It was our first direct effort to provide against a distant and unsubstantial danger, and it failed; but unfortunately we did not take the lesson to heart.

In the meantime the Shah of Persia, instigated by Russia, besieged Herat, but after months of fruitless effort, and in consequence of our sending troops to the Persian Gulf, the Shah at length withdrew his army.

It was not only the hostile efforts of the Shah on Herat in 1838 which were a cause of anxiety to the Indian Government; but, as Kaye writes,[Footnote: Kaye's War in Afghanistan.] 'far out in the distance beyond the mountains of the Hindoo Koosh there was the shadow of a great Northern army, tremendous in its indistinctness, sweeping across the wilds and deserts of Central Asia towards the frontiers of Hindostan.' That great Northern army, as we know now, but did not know then, was the column of Perofski, which had left Orenburg for the attempted conquest of Khiva, but which subsequently perished from hardships and pestilence in the snowy wastes of the Barsuk Desert, north of the Aral.

In view of all the circumstances—of the supposed designs of Russia and Persia, and of the hostility and incessant intrigues in Afghanistan—the Government of India were sorely perplexed, and opinions amongst the authorities widely differed as to the policy to be pursued. Lord Auckland, however, at length decided on the assemblage of a British force for service across the Indus. In his manifesto issued in December 1838 he first alluded to the Burnes mission, and the causes of its failure. He then referred to the claims of Shah Soojah, a former ruler of Afghanistan (who had been living for some years in exile within our territories) and said we had determined, in co-operation with the Sikhs, to restore him to power as Ameer of Cabul.

It was arranged that Shah Soojah should enter Afghanistan with his own troops, such as they were, supported by a British army marching through Scinde and Beloochistan. The Governor-General expressed a hope that tranquillity would thus be established on the frontier, and a barrier formed against external aggression; and he ended by pro claiming that when the object was accomplished the British army would be withdrawn.

This was indeed a momentous decision. The Commander-in-Chief in India, Sir Henry Fane, had already given an adverse opinion, saying that 'every advance you make beyond the Sutlej in my opinion adds to your military weakness.'

On the decision becoming known in England many high authorities, and the public generally, disapproved, of the expedition. The Duke of Wellington said that 'our difficulties would commence where our military successes ended,' and that 'the consequences of crossing the Indus once, to settle a Government in Afghanistan, will be a perennial march, into that country.' The Marquis Wellesley spoke of 'the folly of occupying a land of rocks, sands, deserts, and snow.' Sir Charles Metcalfe from the first protested, and said, 'Depend upon it, the surest way to bring Russia down upon ourselves is for us to cross the Indus and meddle with the countries beyond it.' Mr. Elphinstone wrote: 'If you send 27,000 men up the Bolam to Candahar, and can feed them, I have no doubt you can take Candahar and Cabul and set up Soojah, but as for maintaining him in a poor, cold, strong, and remote country, among a turbulent people like the Afghans, I own it seems to me to be hopeless. If you succeed you will I fear weaken the position against Russia. The Afghans are neutral, and would have received your aid against invaders with gratitude. They will now be disaffected, and glad to join any invader to drive you out.'

Mr. Tucker, of the Court of Directors, wrote to the Duke of Wellington: 'We have contracted an alliance with Shah Soojah, although he does not possess a rood of ground in Afghanistan, nor a rupee which he did not derive from our bounty as a quondam pensioner.' He added, that 'even if we succeed we must maintain him in the government by a large military force, 800 miles from our frontier and our resources.'

The above were strong and weighty opinions and arguments against the rash and distant enterprise on which the Government of India were about to embark. But there is more to be said. Independently of the result in Afghanistan itself, it must be borne in mind that the proposed line of march of the army necessarily led through Scinde and Beloochistan, countries which (whatever their former position may have been) were then independent both of the Ameer and of ourselves.

The force from Bengal, consisting of about 9,500 men of all arms, with 38,000 camp followers, accompanied by Shah Soojah's levy, left Ferozepore in December, and crossing the Indus, arrived at Dadur, the entrance to the Bolam Pass, in March 1839. Difficulties with the Ameers of Scinde at once arose, chiefly as to our passage through their territories; but their remonstrances were disregarded, and they were informed that 'the day they connected themselves with any other Power than England would be the last of their independence, if not of their rule.' [Footnote: Kaye's War in Afghanistan.]

The army then advanced through the Bolam, and reached Quetta on March 26th. But here again obstacles similar in character to those just described occurred, and Sir Alexander Burnes visited the ruler of Beloochistan (the Khan of Khelat), demanding assistance, especially as to supplies of food. The Prince, with prophetic truth, pointed out that though we might restore Shah Soojah, we would not carry the Afghans with us, and would fail in the end. He alluded to the devastation which our march had already caused in the country; but having been granted a subsidy, unwillingly consented to afford us assistance; and the army, leaving possible enemies in its rear, passed on, and reached Candahar without opposition in April. At the end of June it recommenced its march northwards, and Ghuznee having been stormed and captured, our troops without further fighting arrived at Cabul on April 6. Dost Mahomed, deserted for the time by his people, fled northward over the Hindoo Koosh, finding a temporary refuge in Bokhara, and Shah Soojah reigned in his stead.

So far the great expedition had apparently accomplished its object, and the success of the tripartite treaty between ourselves, the Sikhs, and the new Ameer had been successfully carried out, almost entirely, however, by ourselves as the pre-dominant partner.

The time therefore would seem to have arrived when, in fulfilment of Lord Auckland's proclamation, the British army should be withdrawn from Afghanistan. For the moment this appeared to be the case. But in reality it was not so, and our position soon became dangerous, then critical, and at last desperate. In the first place, the long line of communication was liable at any time to be interrupted, as already mentioned; then, again, the arrival of Shah Soojah had excited no enthusiasm; and the very fact that we were foreigners in language, religion and race, rendered our presence hateful to his subjects. In short, the new Ameer was, and continued to be, a mere puppet, supported in authority by British bayonets.

These conditions were apparent from the first day of his arrival, and grew in intensity until the end. Shah Soojah himself soon discovered that his authority over his people was almost nominal; and although he chafed at our continued presence in the country, he also felt that the day of our departure would be the last of his reign, and that our withdrawal was under the circumstances impossible. But the situation was equally complicated from our own point of view. If, as originally promised, the British troops were withdrawn, the failure of the expedition would at once become apparent by the anarchy which would ensue. On the other hand, to retain an army in the far-distant mountains of Afghanistan would not only be a breach of faith, but, while entailing enormous expense, would deprive India of soldiers who might be required elsewhere.

After lengthy consideration, it was decided to reduce the total of our force in the country, while retaining a hold for the present on Cabul, Ghuznee, and Candahar, together with the passes of the Kyber and Bolam. In short, the British army was weakly scattered about in a region of mountains, amongst a hostile people, and with its long lines of communication insufficiently guarded. Both in a military and a political point of view the position was a false and dangerous one.

General Sir John Keane, who was about to return to India, writing at the time, said 'Mark my words, it will not be long before there is here some signal catastrophe.' During the summer of 1840 there were troubles both in the Kyber and Bolam passes. In the former the tribes, incensed at not receiving sufficient subsidies, attacked the outposts and plundered our stores; while in Beloochistan matters were so serious that a British force was sent, and captured Khelat, the Khan being killed, and part of his territory handed over to Shah Soojah. [Footnote: In the life of Sir Robert Sandeman, recently published, it is stated that the alleged treachery of Mehrab Khan, which cost him his life, was on subsequent inquiry not confirmed.] Rumours from Central Asia also added to our anxieties. Although the failure of the Russian attempt on Khiva became known some months later, it excited apprehension at the time amongst our political officers in Cabul. Sir Alexander Burnes, during the winter of 1839, expressed opinions which were curiously inconsistent with each other. 'I maintain,' he said, 'that man to be an enemy to his country who recommends a soldier to be stationed west of the Indus; 'while at the same moment he advocated the advance of our troops over the Hindoo Koosh into Balkh, so as to be ready to meet the Russians in the following May.

Sir William McNaghten, the chief political officer in Cabul, went still further, and in April 1840 not only urged a march on Bokhara, but also contemplated sending a Mission to Kokand, in order, as he said, 'to frustrate the knavish tricks of the Russians in that quarter.'

Our position, however, at that time was sufficiently precarious without adding to our anxieties by distant expeditions in Central Asia, even had the Russians established themselves in the Principalities, which at that time was not the case. Not only was Afghanistan itself seething with treachery and intrigues from one end to the other, but the Sikhs in the Punjaub, our nominal allies, had, since the death of Runjeet Singh, become disloyal and out of hand. Beloochistan was in tumult; the tribes in the Kyber, ever ready for mischief, incessantly threatened our communications; so that we were certainly in no condition to enter upon further dangerous expeditions against distant imaginary foes.

Sir Jasper Nicholls, the Commander-in-Chief, strongly objected to any advance. 'In truth,' he said, 'we are much weaker now than in 1838.'

During the latter months of 1840, and in 1841, matters became steadily worse, and all Afghanistan seemed ripe for revolt. 'We are in a stew here,' wrote Sir William McNaghten in September; 'it is reported that the whole country on this side the Oxus is up in favour of Dost Mahomed, who is certainly advancing in great strength.' Again, in a letter to Lord Auckland, he said 'that affairs in this quarter have the worst possible appearance'—and he quoted the opinion of Sir Willoughby Cotton, that 'unless the Bengal troops are instantly strengthened we cannot hold the country.'

At this critical period, however, Dost Mahomed was heavily defeated at Bamian, on the Hindoo Koosh, voluntarily surrendering shortly afterwards, and for the moment prospects looked brighter; but the clouds soon gathered again, and the end was at hand.

The Governor-General of India had throughout the whole war wisely and steadfastly resisted the proposed further operations in Central Asia; and the Court of Directors in London wrote as follows: 'We pronounce our decided opinion that, for many years to come, the restored monarchy will have need of a British force in order to maintain peace in its own territory, and prevent aggression from without.' And they go on: 'We again desire you seriously to consider which of the two alternatives (a speedy retreat from Afghanistan, or a considerable increase of the military force in that country) you may feel it your duty to adopt. We are convinced that you have no middle course to pursue with safety and with, honour.' The Government of India, hesitating to the last, failed in adopting either of the alternatives.

In November, 1841, Sir Alexander Burnes was treacherously murdered by a mob in Cabul, which was followed by an insurrection, and the defeat of our troops. General Elphinstone, who was in command, writing to Sir W. McNaghten on November 24, said that 'from the want of provisions and forage, the reduced state of our troops, the large number of wounded and sick, the difficulty of defending the extensive and ill-situated cantonment we occupy, the near approach of winter, our communications cut off, no prospect of relief, and the whole country in arms against us, I am of opinion that it is not feasible any longer to maintain our position in this country, and that you ought to avail yourself of the offer to negotiate that has been made to you.'

This was conclusive. Our Envoy early in December met the Afghan chiefs, and agreed that we should immediately evacuate the country, and that Dost Mahomed, who was in exile in India, should return. On December 23, Sir William McNaghten was treacherously murdered at a conference with the Afghan Sirdars, within sight of the British cantonment, and then came the end.

The British force at Cabul, leaving its guns, stores and treasure behind, commenced its retreat on January 6, 1842; but incessantly attacked during its march, and almost annihilated in the Koord Cabul Pass, it ceased to exist as an organised body. General Elphinstone and other officers, invited to a conference by Akbar Khan, were forcibly detained as hostages, and on January 13 a solitary Englishman (Dr. Brydon) arrived at Jellalabad, being, with the exception of a few prisoners, the sole remaining representative of the force.

I have given this short sketch of the first Afghan war because, disastrous as it was, the causes of our failure were due throughout far more to rash and mistaken policy than to any shortcomings of the British troops engaged. Kaye in his 'History' gives a clear summary of its original object and unfortunate results: 'The expedition across the Indus was undertaken with the object of creating in Afghanistan a barrier against encroachment from the west.' 'The advance of the British army was designed to check the aggression of Persia on the Afghan frontier, and to baffle Russian intrigues by the substitution of a friendly for an unfriendly Power in the countries beyond the Indus. After an enormous waste of blood and treasure, we left every town and village of Afghanistan bristling with our enemies. Before the British army crossed the Indus the English name had been honoured in Afghanistan. Some dim traditions of the splendour of Mr. Elphinstone's Mission had been all that the Afghans associated with their thoughts of the English nation, but in their place we left galling memories of the progress of a desolating army.'

The history of the war from first to last deserves careful consideration; and if the lessons taught by it are taken to heart, they will materially assist in determining the principles which, should guide our policy on the North-West frontier of India.

EVENTS PRIOR, AND LEADING UP, TO SECOND AFGHAN WAR

For a few years subsequent to the war, our frontier policy happily remained free from complications, and it will be desirable now to refer shortly to the progress of Russia in Central Asia, and of her conquests of the decaying Principalities of Khiva, Bokhara and Kokand.

Previous to 1847 the old boundary line of Russia south of Orenburg abutted on the great Kirghis Steppe, a zone [Footnote: Parliamentary Papers: Afghanistan, 1878.] (as the late Sir H. Rawlinson told us) of almost uninhabited desert, stretching 2,000 miles from west to east, and nearly 1,000 from north to south, which had hitherto acted as a buffer between Russia and the Mahomedan Principalities below the Aral.

[Footnote: Extract from Quarterly Review, October 1865.]'It was in 1847, contemporaneously with our final conquest of the Punjaub, that the curtain rose on the aggressive Russian drama in Central Asia which is not yet played out. Russia had enjoyed the nominal dependency of the Kirghis-Kozzacks of the little horde who inhabited the western division of the great Steppe since 1730; but, except in the immediate vicinity of the Orenburg line, she had little real control over the tribes. In 1847 -48, however, she erected three important fortresses in the very heart of the Steppe. These important works—the only permanent constructions which had hitherto been attempted south of the line—enabled Russia, for the first time, to dominate the western portion of the Steppe and to command the great routes of communication with Central Asia. But the Steppe forts were after all a mere means to an end; they formed the connecting link between the old frontiers of the empire and the long -coveted line of the Jaxartes, and simultaneously with their erection arose Fort Aralsk, near the embouchure of the river.'

The Russians having thus crossed the great desert tract and established themselves on the Jaxartes (Sir Daria), from that time came permanently into contact with the three Khanates of Central Asia, and their progress since that date has been comparatively easy and rapid.

The Principalities had no military organisation which would enable them to withstand a great Power; their troops and those of Russia were frequently in conflict of late years; but the battles were in a military sense trivial; and the broad result is, that Russia has been for some years predominant throughout the whole region; and her frontiers are now continuous with the northern provinces of both Afghanistan and Persia. It is this latter point which is the important one, so far as we are concerned, but before entering into its details, it will be well to consider the nature of the great country over which Russia now rules.

Until within the last few years our information as to its general character was very limited; but the accounts of numerous recent travellers all concur in describing it as consisting for the most part of sterile deserts, deficient in food, forage, fuel and water. There are a certain number of decayed ancient cities here and there, and there are occasional oases of limited fertility, but the general conditions are as just described. With the exception of the one railway from the Caspian to Samarcand, the means of transport are chiefly pack animals. Speaking roughly, the dominions of Russia in Central Asia, south of Orenburg, may be taken as almost equal in geographical extent to those of our Indian Empire; but there is this striking difference between the two, that whilst the population of India is computed at 250 millions, that of Central Asia, even at the highest computation, is only reckoned at four or five millions, of whom nearly half are nomadic—that is, they wander about, not from choice, but in search of food and pasturage. The extreme scantiness of the population is of itself a rough measure of the general desolation.

The military position of Russia in Central Asia, therefore, is that of a great but distant Power, which during the last fifty years has overrun and taken possession of extended territories belonging to fanatical Mahomedan tribes. The people themselves are, many of them, warlike and hostile; but they are badly armed, have no discipline, training, or leaders, and are not therefore in a position to withstand the advance of regular troops. Consequently Russia is enabled to hold the country with a comparatively small force of scattered detachments, which are, however, supplied with arms, munitions and stores under great difficulties from far distant centres, and her troops are practically incapable of concentration. Indeed the farther they go the weaker they become; the very magnitude of the area being an additional cause of weakness. This is a condition somewhat precarious in itself, and would certainly not appear to be an alarming one as a basis of attack against our Empire, even were India close at hand.

While Russia, however, was completing the subjugation of the Principalities, and advancing her frontiers until they became conterminous with the northern provinces of Afghanistan and Persia, the Government of India, by the great wars of 1843 and 1849, having annexed Scinde and the Punjaub, advanced our frontiers in a similar manner, so that the people both of Beloochistan and Afghanistan, hitherto far remote from our dominions, now became our neighbours.

In the life of Sir Robert Sandeman recently published, a very interesting account is given, not only of the nature of the country along the border, but of the policy pursued for many years with the independent tribes. It says: 'By the conquest of Scinde in 1843, and the annexation of the Punjaub in 1849, the North-West frontier of India was advanced across the river Indus to the foot of the rocky mountains which separate the plains of the Indus valley from the higher plateaus of Afghanistan and Khelat. These mountain ranges formed a vast irregular belt of independent or semi-independent territory, extending from Cashmere southward to the sea near Kurrachee, a total length of about 1,200 miles.' The belt of territory above described was 'inhabited by fierce marauding tribes, often at war with each other, ever and anon harrying the plains of the Punjaub and Scinde, and the constant terror of the trade caravans during their journey through the passes.'

The policy pursued for many years is thus described: 'The disasters of the first Afghan war, and the tragical episode of Khelat, were fresh in men's recollections, and created a strong feeling against political interference with tribes beyond our border'.... 'Accordingly, from the very first, the system of border defence maintained by the Punjaub Government was not purely military, but partly military, partly political and conciliatory. While the passes were carefully watched, every means was taken for the promotion of friendly intercourse.' Roads were made, steamers started on the Indus, and inundation canals developed along the border.

So long as they were friendly the tribesmen had free access to our territory, could hold land, enlist in our army, and make free use of our markets. As a result, the deadly hatred formerly prevailing between the Sikhs and the hill tribes soon disappeared; raids became exceptional; cultivation increased; the bazaars of our frontier stations teemed with Afghans, with trains of laden camels, who at the close of the season returned laden with our goods. Disputes were voluntarily referred by independent tribesmen for the arbitration of British officers. Such, (it is stated in the life of Sir Robert Sandeman) were the results of Lawrence's frontier policy, and no words are required to emphasise these excellent arrangements, which remained in force for many years.

Before leaving this part of the subject, it may be as well to anticipate a little and to allude to the successful part taken by Sir Robert Sandeman in 1876 on his appointment as our agent to the Khan of Khelat. It is important in the first place to mention, that whilst in Afghanistan the tribes all along the frontier were for the most part independent of the Ameer of Cabul, and were ruled by their own 'jirgahs' or councils, in Beloochistan the mode of government was so far different that the chiefs, whilst acknowledging the Khan as their hereditary ruler, were entitled, not only to govern their own tribes, but to take part in the general administration of the country as the constitutional advisers of the paramount chief. The dangers arising from the vicinity of three powerful kingdoms, Persia, Afghanistan, and Scinde, had no doubt led them to perceive the necessity of co-operation, which was established about the middle of the eighteenth century. Although the constitution as above described secured to the confederated tribes nearly a century of prosperity and peaceful government, it so happened that for some years before 1876, owing to the weakness of the then ruler, and partly to turbulence of the chiefs, the government of the country fell into disorder, and the commerce through the Bolam Pass altogether ceased.

From 1872 to 1876 Lord Northbrook was Viceroy of India, and one of his last acts before leaving was the appointment of Colonel Sandeman as our Envoy, with a view to mediate between the Khan and his subordinates, and which proved successful. The principal terms which were finally accepted by the Khan and his tribal chiefs were, that their foreign policy was to be under our guidance, and we were also to be the referee in case of internal disputes; that the commerce of the Bolam was to be opened and protected, the annual subsidy hitherto granted to the Khan of 5,000_l_. being doubled to cover the necessary expenditure; and, finally, that a British Agent with a suitable contingent should be established at Quetta. It is important to observe that the negotiations were conducted throughout in a spirit of conciliation, and that their beneficial results remain in force to the present day.

The policy pursued for many years on the Afghan frontier, although regulated by the same general principles as in Khelat, was not altogether so rapidly accomplished, or so entirely successful. The circumstances were in some degree different and less simple. In the first place the frontier was 800 miles long, and was inhabited by Afghan tribes, who were more predatory and intractable than the Beloochees; they were not only independent of each other, but for the most part acknowledged no allegiance to the Ameer of Cabul. Border disputes therefore had to be settled with individual chiefs; and no opportunity was offered for our mediation in internal feuds, or for joint agreement on external policy, as was so successfully accomplished by Sandeman in Beloochistan. There was no general federation with which we could enter into negotiation. As a consequence, we were compelled to maintain a large force and fortified posts along the frontier; and many punitive expeditions became necessary from time to time against lawless offending tribes. Still, on the whole, and considering the difficulties of the situation, the policy of conciliation, subsidies, and of non- interference with their internal affairs, gradually succeeded; raids once chronic became exceptional, and were dealt with rather as matters of frontier policy than of war. [Footnote: See Parliamentary Papers: Afghanistan, 1878, page 30, and Beloochistan, No. 3, 1878.]

It must also be remembered, as an additional complication, that in annexing the Punjaub, although it is essentially the country of the Sikhs, who are Hindoos, the inhabitants of the trans-Indus districts are for the most part what are termed Punjaubee Mussulmen, that is, Afghans, in race, religion and language.

From what has been said as to our dealings with the border tribes, it will be evident that while our difficulties were continuous and often serious, still, they were chiefly local; and that the defence of the Empire on that frontier against foreign aggression depended in a great measure on our relations with the ruler of Afghanistan itself. When Dost Mahomed, after the great war, returned in 1843 to his former position as Ameer of that distracted country, it was hardly to be expected that, although acquiescing in his reinstatement, we should be regarded by him in a friendly light; still, some years passed away without any important change in our relative positions, one way or the other.

In 1855, Lord Dalhousie was Governor-General, and a treaty was made with Dost Mahomed, by which both parties agreed to respect each other's territories. In January, 1857, a still more important one followed. We were then once more at war with Persia; and at a meeting between Sir John Lawrence and the Ameer, an agreement was entered into that Dost Mahomed, acting in co-operation with us, should receive 10,000_l_. a month for military purposes, to continue during the war; that English officers should reside in his country temporarily, to keep the Indian Government informed, but not to interfere with the administration, and that when peace ensued they should be withdrawn, and a native agent alone remain as our representative. [Footnote: In view of the strong objection to the presence of English officers in Afghanistan, Sir John Lawrence intimated to the Viceroy of India that he had given an assurance to Dost Mahomed that it should not be enforced unless imperatively necessary.]

It is important to note that this friendly treaty was made at Peshawur, just before the great Mutiny, and that the Ameer, though urged by his people to attack us in our hour of danger, remained faithful, and would not allow them to cross the border.

Dost Mahomed died in June, 1863, and for some years after his death family feuds and intestine wars occurred as to his successor, during which we carefully abstained from interference, and were prepared to acknowledge the de facto ruler. Ultimately, in 1868, his son Shere Ali established his authority in Afghanistan, and was acknowledged accordingly. Lord Lawrence was then the Viceroy, and in a despatch to the Secretary of State expressed his views as regards the advances of Russia. After pointing out that they were now paramount in Central Asia, he suggested a mutual agreement as to our respective spheres and relations with the tribes and nations with whom we were now both in contact, and he went on to welcome the civilising effect of Russian government over the wild tribes of the Steppes, and pointed out that if Russia were assured of our loyal feeling in these matters, she would have no jealousy in respect of our alliance with the Afghans.

The Secretary of State (Sir Stafford Northcote) replied 'that the conquests which Russia had made, and apparently is still making, in Central Asia, appear to be the natural result of the circumstances in which she finds herself placed, and to afford no ground whatever for representations indicative of suspicion or alarm on the part of this country.' It is a great misfortune that such sensible, conciliatory views did not continue to guide our policy in the events which a few years later led us into the second great war in Afghanistan.

Shere Ali did not inherit the great qualities of his father, and was also somewhat discontented that we had not abetted his cause during the internal troubles in Afghanistan. However, in 1869 he met Lord Mayo at Umballa, and after careful discussion it was agreed that we should abstain from sending British officers across the frontier and from interfering in Afghan affairs; that our desire was that a strong, friendly, and independent Government should be established in that country. It was further decided to give Shere Ali considerable pecuniary assistance, and presents of arms from time to time. The Ameer, while gratified at these results, wished us also to give a dynastic pledge as to his lineal descendants, which, however, was not acceded to. In 1873 Lord Northbrook was Viceroy of India, and a further conference took place at Simla with the Ameer's Prime Minister, chiefly as to the northern Afghan frontier in Badakshan and Wakkan, which were at the time somewhat uncertain, and a matter of dispute with Russia.

This somewhat delicate question was, however, settled in a friendly manner by Lord Granville, then Secretary of State for Foreign Affairs. Prince Gortschakoff's final despatch to him on the subject was as follows: [Footnote: Central Asia, 1873—c. 699.] 'The divergence which existed in our views was with regard to the frontiers assigned to the dominion of Shere Ali. The English Government includes within them Badakshan and Wakkan, which according to our views enjoyed a certain independence. Considering the difficulty experienced in establishing the facts in all their details in those distant parts; considering the greater facilities which the British Government possesses for collecting precise detail, and above all considering our wish not to give to this question of detail greater importance than is due to it, we do not refuse to accept the boundary line laid down by England. We are the more inclined to this act of courtesy as the English Government engages to use all its influence with Shere Ali in order to induce him to maintain a peaceful attitude, as well as to insist on his giving up all measures of aggression or further conquest. This influence is indisputable. It is based, not only on the material and moral ascendency of England, but also on the subsidies for which Shere Ali is indebted to her. Such being the case, we see in this assurance a real guarantee for the maintenance of peace.'

Prince Gortschakoff admitted more than once that the Emperor of Russia looked upon Afghanistan as completely outside the sphere of Russian influence, and within that of ours; at the same time, claiming similar independence for Russia in Central Asia.

During the next few years, subsequent to the Simla conference, Shere Ali, though he had received considerable assistance from us, both in money and arms, was not altogether satisfied, and one or two incidents occurred during that period which gave him umbrage. Lord Northbrook, the Viceroy in 1875, was not unaware of the somewhat cold and capricious spirit of the Ameer, but in writing to London he pointed out that Shere Ali's situation was difficult, not only from the risk of revolution at home, but also of attack from abroad, but that on the whole he was to be relied on.

A change, however, was coming over the scene, and our policy reverted from conciliation to compulsion. It was a critical period in the history of frontier policy, and demands careful consideration.

It must not be forgotten that although amongst those best qualified to judge the majority had long been opposed to advance and conquest in territories beyond our North-West frontier, and entertained but little fear of Russian aggressive power, still there were others—men of long experience, who had filled high positions in India—who held different views; and it is probable that not only successive British Governments, but the public generally, who have no time for carefully weighing the diverse aspects of the subject, were influenced sometimes one way, sometimes another. In the many difficulties connected with our world-wide Empire this must always be more or less the case. For instance, the late Sir H. Rawlinson, a few years before the second Afghan war, took a very alarmist view of the progress of Russia, not only in Central Asia but also in Asia Minor. He considered that her advance from Orenburg was only part of one great scheme of invasion; and he averred that the conquest of the Caucasus had given her such a strong position that there was no military or physical obstacle to the continuous march of Russia from the Araxes to the Indus. [Footnote: Parliamentary Papers, Afghanistan, 1878.] He described it as the unerring certainty of a law of nature. But, throughout, he ignores distances, blots out the mountains, deserts, and arid plains of Persia and Afghanistan, and takes no account of the warlike races who would bar the path. It requires a very large map to embrace all the details of this widespread strategy.

Some account has already been given of the weakness, in a military point of view, of Russia in Central Asia, and of the distance of her scattered troops from the main resources of the Empire. But, in addition, it must be remembered that the mountains of Afghanistan also form a natural and enduring barrier against a further advance. The great Hindoo Koosh range, running all along the northern part of that country, forms indeed the real scientific frontier between the two Empires, the few passes over its snowy crests ranging from 12,000 to 18,000 feet high, and only open for a few months in the year.

Another supposed line of advance for a Russian army, namely by the Pamirs, has of late years been brought forward; but its main features are more discouraging than those of any other. This elevated region consists of a mass of bare snow-capped mountains attaining elevations of over 25,000 feet, intersected by plateaux almost as devoid of vegetation as the mountains themselves. The lakes are about 12,000 feet above the sea, the population is scanty, and consists chiefly of nomads in search of food and pasture during the short summer; so that although the Russians might, if unopposed, possibly move in small isolated detachments carrying their own food and munitions over the Pamirs, it would only be to lose themselves in the gorges of the Himalayas.

The conditions above mentioned are for the most part permanent. Russia may not, and probably has not, any intention of trying to invade and conquer India—but she has not the power, which is a far more important consideration.

To return to the position of affairs previous to the second Afghan war. [Footnote: See Afghanistan, 1878, published by Secretary of State for India, p. 128 et seq.] Early in 1875, Lord Northbrook, the Governor -General, received a despatch from the Government at home, pointing out that the information received from Afghanistan, not only in respect to internal intrigues but also as regards the influence of foreign Powers, was scanty, and not always trustworthy. He was, therefore, instructed to procure the assent of the Ameer to the establishment of a British Agency at Herat, and also at Candahar.

The Viceroy of India and his Council having consulted various experienced officers on the subject, replied in June, that in their opinion the present time and circumstances were unsuitable for taking the initiative. They pointed out that the Sirdars and many of the people of Afghanistan would strongly object, and that in the Ameer's somewhat insecure position he could not afford to disregard their feelings in the matter. They advised patience and conciliation.

In November 1875 a second despatch was received from England, reiterating the necessity of more complete information as to Afghanistan, especially in view of recent Russian advances in Central Asia; and the Viceroy was directed to send a Mission to Cabul without delay, to confer with the Ameer on Central Asia, and requesting that British officers should be placed on the frontier to watch the course of events.

The Government of India, in January 1876, again urged the undesirability of forcing the hands of the Ameer, and pointed out that his objections to English officers were not from a feeling of disloyalty, and that to force his hands was not desirable. They did not apprehend any desire of interference on the part of Russia, and they concluded by alluding to the careful conciliatory policy carried out by Lords Canning, Lawrence, and Mayo, as giving the best promise of peace, and satisfactory results in Afghanistan. Consequently they deprecated the proposed action by the Home Government in forcing British officers upon Shere Ali. In April 1876 Lord Northbrook quitted India, and was succeeded by Lord Lytton; and a further reply from Lord Salisbury, the Secretary of State for India, was received by the Viceroy. It reiterated that the Government at home considered our trans-frontier relations unsatisfactory; that permanent British Agencies should be established in Afghanistan; and that we were willing to afford the Ameer material support against unprovoked aggression, our object being to maintain a strong and friendly Power in that country. The despatch went on to say that should the Ameer decline to meet our request, he should be informed that he was isolating himself from us at his peril.

The next step was taken in May, when the Ameer was invited to receive a special Mission, which he politely declined. In October our native Agent at Cabul came to Simla and had an interview with Lord Lytton, who reiterated the demands of the British Government, pointing out that in the event of a refusal there was nothing to prevent our joining Russia in wiping Afghanistan out of the map altogether, of which Shere Ali was duly informed. In January 1877 a final effort was made to come to terms, and Sir Lewis Pelly and the Afghan Prime Minister, Noor Mahomed, had a conference at Peshawur. The first, and indeed the only point discussed, was the demand that British representatives should reside in Afghanistan, which was a sine qua non. Noor Mahomed pathetically pleaded that Lords Lawrence, Mayo, and Northbrook, successive Viceroys, had all in turn promised that this should not be insisted on; and he ended by saying that Shere Ali would rather perish than submit. It was evident that further discussion was useless, and the conference was closed; Noor Mahomed, who was ill, dying shortly afterwards. In March 1877 our native Agent at Cabul was withdrawn, and direct communication with Shere Ali ceased.

I have given the above resume of the correspondence in 1875-77, and of the abortive efforts to induce the Ameer to comply with our demands, because it is evident that if he continued to resist compulsion must almost inevitably ensue. At about the same time, Quetta, in the Bolam, was occupied by a considerable British force, which was naturally regarded as a threat on Afghanistan. A concentration of troops also took place in the Northern Punjaub, and preparations were made for the construction of bridges over the Indus. All these were indications of coming war. It must also be noted that our relations with Russia in Europe were much strained at the time, so that probably the preparations in India were in some degree due to the apprehension of war in other parts of the world.

In the summer of 1878 a Russian Envoy arrived at Cabul, which under the circumstances is hardly to be wondered at. Some months however elapsed, and it was not until November 1878 that war was declared. Lord Lytton, the Viceroy, in his proclamation stated: 'That for ten years we had been friendly to Shere Ali; had assisted him with money and arms; and had secured for him formal recognition of his northern frontier by Russia.' It went on to state, that in return he had requited us with active ill-will; had closed the passes and allowed British traders to be plundered; and had endeavoured to stir up religious hatred against us. It then pointed out that whilst refusing a British Mission he had received one from Russia; and ended by saying that we had no quarrel with the Afghans, but only with Shere Ali himself.

From official correspondence published subsequently [Footnote: Parliamentary Papers, Afghanistan, 1881, No. 2.—c. 2811.] it appeared that in entering Afghanistan our chief object at the outset was to establish what was called a strategical triangle, by the occupation of Cabul, Ghuznee and Jellalabad; and it was stated that by holding this position, entrenched behind a rampart of mountains, we should have the power of debouching on the plains of the Oxus against Russia in Central Asia! 'It is difficult,' said Lord Lytton, 'to imagine a more commanding strategical position.' The events of the war, however, soon put an end to this somewhat fanciful strategy.

In November 1878 the British forces entered the country by three main routes, the Kyber, the Koorum, and the Bolam, and hard fighting at once ensued on the two northern ones. The results were immediate: Shere Ali fled northwards, and died soon after. His son, Yakoob Khan, assumed temporarily the position of Ameer, but in the convulsed state of the country lie possessed little real power or authority. In May, 1879, he met the British authorities at Gundamuk, and after considerable discussion signed a treaty, the chief points of which were as follows:— The foreign affairs of Afghanistan were to be under our guidance; and we undertook to support the Ameer against foreign aggression; British agents were to reside in the country; the Koorum, Pisheen, and Sibi Valleys were assigned to the British Government; and finally, Yakoob Khan was to receive an annual subsidy of 60,000_l_.

So far, it would appear as if the campaign had at once realised the main objects of British policy; but tragic events rapidly followed, active hostilities were resumed, and the Treaty of Gundamuk became mere waste paper.

As a first result of the treaty, Sir Louis Cavagnari [Footnote: Afghanistan, 1881, No. 1.] was appointed our Envoy, and accompanied by a few officers and a small escort, arrived at Cabul in July, being received in a friendly manner by the Ameer; although influences adverse to his presence in the capital soon became apparent. Suddenly, on September 3, the British Residency was attacked by several Afghan regiments, and after a desperate resistance, Cavagnari and the whole of his officers and escort perished.

This deplorable event, of course, upset all previous arrangements, and led to an immediate resumption of hostilities. Our troops at once advanced and captured Cabul, Yakoob Khan voluntarily abdicating and becoming an exile in India. Ghuznee also was occupied shortly afterwards by our advance from Candahar.

The Government of India, in a despatch in January, 1880, pointed out that, in view of the complete change in the political situation, it was necessary, in the first place, fully to establish our military position in the country. They acknowledged that the hopes entertained of establishing a strong, friendly, and independent kingdom on our frontier had collapsed; and that Afghanistan had fallen to pieces at the first blow, its provinces being now disconnected and masterless. In view of these unexpected results, they went on to recommend the permanent separation of the provinces under separate rulers; and having regard to the special difficulties connected with Herat, advocated its being handed over to Persia!

This was indeed a policy of despair!

Lord Hartington, who had become Secretary of State for India, writing in May, 1880, summed up the situation as follows :—'It appears that as the result of two successful campaigns, of the employment of an enormous force, and of the expenditure of large sums of money, all that has yet been accomplished has been the disintegration of the State which it was desired to see strong, friendly and independent; the assumption of fresh and unwelcome liabilities in regard to one of its provinces, and a condition of anarchy throughout the remainder of the country.'

Long and careful consideration was naturally given to the solution of the difficulty in which this country found itself owing to the untoward circumstances just related. Two important decisions were however ultimately arrived at: [Footnote: Afghanistan, 1881, No. 1.]

1. That authority in Afghanistan, and the unity of its provinces, should as far as possible be restored by the appointment of a new Ameer; and Abdul Rahman, a nephew of Shere Ali, who had been for twelve years an exile in Bokhara, was invited to Cabul, and was supported by us in assuming the title.

The chief conditions were, that his foreign policy was to be under our guidance, that no English officers were to reside as our representatives in Afghanistan, and that he was to receive a subsidy.

2. That the British troops should be withdrawn as soon as the pacification of the country would permit. This decision was recommended not only by the Viceroy, the Marquis of Ripon, but by the higher officers who had held command during the war. Sir Donald Stewart, who was in chief command, and Sir Frederick Roberts, both, concurred in our withdrawal from the country; the Kyber Pass was to be held by subsidised tribes, and the Koorum Valley to be altogether abandoned; the independence of the tribes being in each case recognised. Sir John Watson, who was in command in that valley, pointed out that as a route from India into Afghanistan it was practically useless. As a further argument in favour of withdrawal, it may be well to allude to the fact that the men of our native regiments were sick of serving in Afghanistan, far away from their homes, and that it would be impolitic to keep them there.

Some differences of opinion existed as to whether we should relinquish possession of Candahar; but as it was 400 miles from the Indus, in a foreign country, and as our remaining there would not only be hateful to the Afghans, but in a military sense would be dangerous and costly, its final abandonment was decided on; the valley of Pisheen, between Candahar and Quetta, being alone retained by the British Government.

So ended the great war of 1878-80. At its close we had over 70,000 men in Afghanistan, or on the border in reserve; and even then we really only held the territory within range of our guns. The whole country had been disintegrated and was in anarchy; whilst the total cost of the war exceeded twenty millions sterling, being about the same amount as had been expended in the former great war of 1839-41.

The military operations in themselves had been conducted throughout with great skill in a most difficult country, and the troops, both British and Native, had proved themselves admirable soldiers; but as regards the policy which led us into war, it appears to have been as unjust in principle as it was unfortunate in result. The facts, however, speak for themselves.

FRONTIER POLICY SINCE SECOND AFGHAN WAR, INCLUDING EXPEDITION TO CHITRAL

The reaction after the war naturally inclined the authorities in both countries to leave frontier policy alone, at all events for the time. Our professed object for years had been to make Afghanistan strong, friendly, and independent. The first had certainly not been accomplished, and the other two were doubtful. Still, by patience, conciliation, and subsidies, we might hope in the course of time that the wounds we had inflicted would gradually be healed, and a more stable condition ensue. For a short period it was so; but then the old bugbear of Russian advance over the dreary wastes of Central Asia again supervened, and exercised its malign influence on our policy.

In 1881 and the following years, Russia, whilst completing her conquests, and improving her communications in the south-western part of Central Asia, became involved in somewhat prolonged hostilities with the Tekke-Turcomans, ending in their subjugation, and in the occupation of the long, desolate strip of country extending eastwards from the Caspian, which had hitherto been independent. A railway was gradually constructed from the vicinity of Kras-novodsk, on the Caspian, towards Samarcand. Merv, formerly a city of importance, but of late a mere village in the desert, was also occupied. These acquisitions of Russia, accomplished in districts far removed from India, would not appear to involve any special consideration on our part; but as the southern frontiers of Russia thus became conterminous for a long distance with Northern Persia, and also with some districts of Afghanistan, their new position was regarded as possibly involving designs against our Indian Empire, and remonstrances were made by us, more especially as regards the occupation of Merv.[Footnote: Central

Asia, No. 2, 1885.]
In a strategical point of view the question would not appear to be of much importance, and would probably have dropped; but early in 1885 the Russians attacked and drove the Afghan troops out of Penjdeh, a small, hitherto almost unknown village in the desert. It was a high-handed measure, and the relations between the two Governments, British and Russian, which were already rather strained, became critical, and war at one moment appeared to be almost inevitable.

It is not necessary, nor would it be desirable, now to recapitulate the details of this serious crisis; because, happily, owing to the prudence exercised by both Governments, the danger gradually passed away, a Joint Commission being agreed on, to meet on the frontier, and to report as to its delimitation. It may, however, be as well to mention that it seems rather doubtful whether Penjdeh at the time absolutely belonged to Afghanistan. Frontiers in the East are proverbially uncertain and shifting, and in our own official maps, not very long before the occurrences in question, it was marked as outside the Afghan border. Colonel Stewart, reporting in 1884 on the northern frontier of Afghanistan, and alluding to Penjdeh, said that it was inhabited by Turcomans, and he thus described the position: 'The state of affairs seems to have been that the Turcomans acknowledged that they were squatting on Afghan land, and were liable to pay taxes, and each year they paid something as an acknowledgment of Afghan rights; but so long as this was done, the Afghans looked upon them as a protection against the Tekke further north, and left them very much to themselves.'

The appointment of a Joint Commission of Russian and British officers to delimit the northern frontiers of Afghanistan proved of great value, not only in gaining information regarding districts hitherto but little known, but also because its conjoint work tended to engender feelings of respect and goodwill between the two nations concerned.

Its labours commenced in the autumn of 1885, and the report of Sir West Ridgeway, the British Commissioner, is full of interest and encouragement. In an article in the 'Nineteenth Century' of October, 1887, on the completion of his work, he gives some details of the country, and also of the position of Russia in Central Asia, which are worth quoting. As to the Afghan border he says: 'The three or four hundred miles of country through which the new north-western frontier of Afghanistan runs is a sandy, treeless, waterless desert, except where it is traversed from south to north by the Heri-Rood, the Murghab and the Oxus. The only cultivable ground is on the banks of these rivers; but in spring time, after the winter snows have melted, the intervening plains afford good grazing for sheep.' But perhaps the most important part of his article is his view of the position of Russia in Central Asia: 'If any Russian general,' he writes, 'were so reckless as to attempt the invasion of India, and relying on the single line of lightly constructed rails which connects the Caspian with the Oxus, and which are liable in summer to be blocked by the moving sands of the desert, and in winter by the falling snows of Heaven—if, relying on this frail and precarious base, he were to move an army through the barren plains bordering the Oxus, and leaving in his rear the various hostile and excited races of Central Asia, he were to cross the difficult passes of the Hindoo Koosh, and entangle his army in the barren mountain homes of the fanatical and treacherous Afghan, then indeed our fortunate generals may well congratulate themselves that the Lord has delivered the enemy into their hand....'

Whilst, however, his conclusions as to the military weakness of Russia in that part of the world are clear and decisive enough, he at the same time does full justice to the good work which she is carrying out in that vast area. He says: 'Hitherto Russia's advance in Central Asia has been the triumph of civilisation. Wherever she has planted her flag slavery has ceased to exist. This was keenly brought home to us in the course of our travels. For hundreds of miles before we reached Herat we found the country desolated and depopulated by Turcoman raids, while even in the Herat valley we continually came across the fathers and brothers of men who had been carried off from their peaceful fields by man-stealing Turcomans, and sold into slavery many hundred miles away. All this has ceased since the Russian occupation of Merv; the cruel slave trade has been stamped out....'

Lord Salisbury, speaking in 1887, at the conclusion of the frontier delimitation, happily described the situation as follows: 'I value the settlement for this reason—not that I attach much importance to the square miles of desert land with which we have been dealing, and which probably after ten generations of mankind will not yield the slightest value to any human being: but the settlement indicates on both sides that spirit which in the two Governments is consistent with continued peace. There is abundant room for both Governments, if they would only think so....'

What a pity that some statesman could not have persuaded England to that effect fifty years before!

During the next few years no events of special importance occurred to affect our general frontier policy in India, so far as Russia and Afghanistan proper are concerned. The ample information we now possess of the relative power and position of each country, and the experience gained in bygone wars, enable us to form a correct judgment of the great strength of our Empire in the East; and it is to be hoped that in the future we shall hear less of those alarmist views which have so frequently led us into erroneous policy and untoward expeditions.

Russia and England are now, happily, on friendly terms, and Abdul Rahman, the Ameer of Cabul, although his position is difficult in the midst of a turbulent people, has proved himself a loyal neighbour.

But another cloud has appeared on the horizon, and our troubles with the intervening frontier tribes are now apparently worse than ever. From accounts already given of those who dwell along the border, it is evident that although our differences with them, during past years, have been frequent and often serious, they have been more or less of a local character. Troublesome as our neighbours have proved, still they have no power of inflicting serious injury, or of endangering our rule. Under these circumstances, the best policy, whilst firmly repressing their predatory instincts, is to leave them alone.

In the absence of full official information as to the origin of recent difficulties, which have culminated in the present frontier war, it is only possible to speak in general terms. It may be mentioned, in the first place, that owing to the uncertain line of demarcation between the territories of the Ameer of Cabul and those of his independent tribal neighbours, constant feuds and local hostilities occurred from time to time in the mountains; and with a view of defining their respective spheres, the Government of India, in 1893, sent a Mission to Cabul for the purpose. This in itself would appear to have been a reasonable step; and the 'Durand Agreement' which ensued (but which has not been published) would, it was hoped, tend to a cessation of conflicts between the Ameer's subjects and their neighbours. But there is a further aspect of the question. So far as is known, not only were the respective borders laid down, but it is understood that in many cases the intervening tribes are now assumed to be what is termed 'within the sphere of British influence.' In maps recently published, presumably with some authority, vast mountainous districts are now included in this somewhat mysterious phrase. For instance, the Koorum Valley, the Samana Range, the countries of the Afredis and the Mohmunds, the districts of Chitral, Bajour, Dir, Swat, Bonair, and others, are all included within it; and in many instances fortified positions, occupied by British troops, are to be found either within or along their borders.

Surely this opens out a wide question, and it would be interesting to know whether, in the discussions at Cabul, the chiefs of the intervening tribes were present, and whether they acquiesced, not only in the new boundaries, but also in being included as within our sphere of influence? It is evident it should have been a tripartite, and not a dual, agreement. It is perfectly well known, and has been proved by long experience, that these frontier tribes value their independence and liberties, beyond everything else, and will not submit peacefully to interference; and if they were not consulted in the arrangements just described, we may begin to trace the origin of the present crisis.

Although, as I have explained, we are unable, from want of official information, to deal fully with, the larger topic of recent border policy, we have, at all events, ample details as regards the Chitral question in the

Parliamentary Papers published [Footnote: North-West Frontier, Chitral, 1895.] in 1895. It appears that so long ago as 1876 the ruler of Chitral voluntarily tendered his allegiance to the Maharajah of Cashmere, and endeavoured, but without success, to persuade the neighbouring chiefs of Swat, Bajour, and Dir, to follow his example. Now Chitral and Cashmere are not only far apart, but are separated by lofty mountain ranges, inhabited by other tribes, so that this sudden offer of vassalage seems rather inexplicable. It transpired, however, a few years afterwards, that his real motive in seeking the friendship of Cashmere was due to his fear of aggression by the Ameer of Cabul.[Footnote: Ibid, page 46.]

The Government of India at the time encouraged this somewhat sentimental friendship, and in order to obtain influence over the intervening tribes established a fort at Gilgit, in an almost inaccessible position, not far from the snowy crests of the Hindoo Koosh. The position, however, proved to be costly, and also dangerous from unfriendly neighbours, and, as after three years' experience no special object was attained, it was withdrawn in 1881.

In 1889 the old fears of possible Russian aggression again revived, and Gilgit was reoccupied with a strong detachment of Cashmere troops, accompanied by several English officers. The Government of India pointed out that the development of Russian military resources in Asia rendered it necessary to watch the passes over the mountains, in order to prevent what was called a coup de main from the north. In short, they dreaded the march of a Russian army over the Pamirs and the Hindoo Koosh —a region where Nature has constructed for us perhaps one of the most formidable frontiers in the world.

Friendship with the ruler of Chitral was also cultivated. He was given an annual subsidy, and a present of 500 Sniders; being visited also by English officers. It was even contemplated at the time to construct a direct road from his capital to our frontier near Peshawur; but as he was suspicious, and as his neighbours in Swat, Bajour, and others would probably have objected, the suggestion was happily postponed.

In October 1892 the ruler of Chitral died, and after the usual family contests and intrigues, Nizamul-Mulk, his son, established his authority in the country.

In January, 1893, Dr. Robertson arrived at Chitral as our representative, accompanied by two officers and fifty Sikhs. Although he was received in a friendly manner by the new ruler, his account of the state of affairs in April was discouraging and ominous. He wrote: 'We seem to be on a volcano here. Matters are no longer improving; the atmosphere of Chitral is one of conspiracy and intrigue.' A few weeks later he gave a more cheerful account, and although he described the people as fickle, he considered that Englishmen were safe. It became evident, however, that the Nizam-ul-Mulk was weak and unpopular, and Dr. Robertson described the country as 'in a distracted state, and torn by factions.'

The reports of our Agent, in short, would seem to prove that he was in a false and dangerous position, with a small escort, far away in the mountains, about 200 miles from our frontier.

In January, 1895, the Nizam was murdered by his brother, and the whole country at once again fell into anarchy. Dr. Robertson, who had been temporarily absent, but had returned in February, was besieged in a fort, with his escort, which, however, had been increased to about 290 men. The crisis had come at last, and there was no time to spare.

A strong force under Sir Robert Low was assembled at Peshawur, and crossed the frontier on April 1. It must be pointed out that, in proceeding to Chitral, the British troops had necessarily to pass through a difficult mountainous country inhabited by independent tribes; and the Government of India issued a proclamation in which they pointed out that their sole object 'is to put an end to the present and to prevent any future unlawful aggression on Chitral territory, and that as soon as this object has been attained the force would be withdrawn.' The proclamation went on to say, that the Government 'have no intention of permanently occupying any territory through which Mura Khan's misconduct may now force them to pass, or of interfering with the independence of the tribes.'

The military operations were conducted with great skill and rapidity, and Dr. Robertson's small garrison, which at one time had been hard pressed, was saved: a small force under Colonel Kelly, which had left Gilgit, having by a daring and successful march arrived just before the main body from Peshawur.

The short campaign having thus accomplished its object, the gradual withdrawal of the British troops in accordance with the proclamation would seem to have been a natural sequence. In the weak, distracted state of the country, and in the assumed necessity of not losing our influence in those distant regions, the Government of India, however, considered that a road from our frontier to Chitral should be made, and certain positions retained in order to guard it. This vital question having been carefully considered at home, the Secretary of State for India, on June 13, 1895, telegraphed to the Viceroy that her Majesty's Government regretted they were unable to concur in the proposal. He went on to say that no 'military force or European Agent shall be kept at Chitral; that Chitral should not be fortified; and that no road shall be made between Peshawur and Chitral.' He added that all positions beyond our frontier should be evacuated as speedily as circumstances allowed.

It so happened that within a few days of this important decision a change of Government occurred at home, and the question was reconsidered; and on August 9, fresh instructions were telegraphed to India, by which it was ordered that British troops should be stationed at the Malakund Pass, leading into Swat, and that other posts up to, and including, Chitral, should also be held, and a road made through the country. In short the previous decision was entirely reversed.

Before going further it may be as well to point out that this is no mere question between one political party and another. It goes far beyond that, and we may feel assured that in considering the subject, both Governments were actuated by a desire to do what was considered best in the interests of the Indian Empire.

Still, it is I think impossible not to regard the ultimate decision as very unfortunate, and as likely to lead to serious consequences. In a mere military point of view, it was a repetition of the policy pursued of recent years of establishing isolated military posts in countries belonging to others, or in their vicinity; inevitably tending to aggravate the tribes, and which in time of trouble, instead of increasing our strength, are and have been the cause of anxiety to ourselves. Therefore, not only as a matter of policy, but in a purely military sense, the arrangement was dangerous.

I would further observe that many officers, both civil and military, men of the highest character and long experience in the Punjaub and its borders, did not hesitate to express their opinions at the time, that retribution would speedily follow; and their anticipations appear now to have been verified. Suddenly, not many weeks ago, the people of Swat, who were said to be friendly, violently attacked our position on the Malakund, losing, it is said, 3,000 men in the attempt; and also nearly captured a fortified post a few miles distant at Chakdara. Not only that, but this unexpected outbreak was followed by hostilities on the part of the tribes in Bajour, and by the Mohmunds north, of Peshawur, and also by the Afredis, who, subsidised by us, had for years guarded the celebrated Kyber. Again, the tribes of the Samana range, and others to the west of Kohat, rose in arms; and a very large force of British troops had to be pushed forward in all haste to quell this great combined attack on the part of our neighbours. General Sir Neville Chamberlain, perhaps the greatest living authority on frontier questions, has written quite recently, pointing out that never previously had there been a semblance of unity of action amongst the different tribesmen.[Footnote: Saturday Review, 30th Oct. 1897.]

There surely must have been some very strong feeling of resentment and injustice which brought so many tribesmen for the first time to combine in opposition to what they evidently considered an invasion of their country. As regards the Afredis, who are spoken of as treacherous and faithless, it must be borne in mind that in 1881 we specially recognised their independence,[Footnote: Afghanistan No. 1, 1881, page 57.] and have ever since subsidised them for the special purpose of guarding the commerce through the Kyber; a duty which they have faithfully carried out until the present summer. Lord Lytton, who was Viceroy when the arrangement was proposed at the end of the war, wrote in 1880 [Footnote: Ibid, page 62.]—'I sincerely hope that the Government of India will not be easily persuaded to keep troops permanently stationed in the Kyber. I feel little doubt that such a course would tend rather to cause trouble than to keep order. Small bodies of troops would be a constant provocation to attack; large bodies would die like flies....'

'I believe that the Pass tribes themselves, if properly managed, will prove the best guardians of the Pass, and be able, as well as willing, to keep it open for us, if we make it worth their while to do so....' Many of these very men, and those of other tribes on the frontier, have for years enlisted in our ranks, and have proved to be good soldiers. I repeat that some strong cause must have influenced them suddenly to break out into war.

Until the present military operations have been brought to a close, and until full official information has been given of the circumstances which have led to them, it is not possible to pronounce a final judgment; still, it seems to me, that we have strong grounds for believing that the border policy of late years has in many instances been too aggressive and regardless of the rights of the tribes; and that the course finally pursued of the retention of fortified posts through Swat and Bajour to Chitral, has been the ultimate cause which has excited the people against us, and produced so great and costly a border war. It must also not be forgotten, that even now we are merely on the fringe, as it were, of the question; and that if we persist in forcing ourselves forward, we shall have many a costly campaign to undertake far away in distant, little-known regions, more difficult and more inaccessible even than those in which we now find ourselves.

On the whole it appears to me that we should as far as possible withdraw our isolated posts, so many of which, are either within the tribal country or along its borders. It is sometimes argued that any withdrawal on our part would have a demoralising effect on the tribes, who would ascribe our retirement to inability to maintain our positions. [Footnote: Chitral, 1895, page 62.] The best reply will perhaps be to quote the words of Lord Hartington, when under similar circumstances it was decided in 1881 to retire from Candahar. He said: [Footnote: Afghanistan, No. 1, 1881, page 92.] 'The moral effect of a scrupulous adherence to declarations which have been made, and a striking and convincing proof given to the people and princes of India that the British Government have no desire for further annexation of territory, could not fail to produce a most salutary effect, in removing the apprehensions, and strengthening the attachment of our native allies throughout India, and on our frontiers....'

These remarks may now be brought to a close. My object throughout has been to give an historical summary of the various wars and expeditions in which we have been engaged during the present century on the North -

West frontier of India; and of the causes which have led to them. My observations are founded on Parliamentary official papers, and on other works of authority; and I hope they may prove useful to the public, who have not, as a rule time to study the intricate details of this difficult subject. I have endeavoured to prove that the tribes on the frontier, and the people of Afghanistan, have no real power of injuring our position in India; and turbulent as they may be, a policy of patience, conciliation, and subsidies, is far more likely to attain our object than incessant costly expeditions into their mountains. Our influence over them is already great, and is increasing year by year. By carefully maintaining the principles I have sketched out, we shall gradually obtain their friendship, and also their support, should other dangers ever threaten our dominions.

We are the rulers of a great Empire in the East, with its heavy duties and responsibilities, and in devoting ourselves to the welfare of the millions under our sway, and in developing the resources of the country, we shall do far more for the happiness of the people and the security of the Empire than by squandering our finances in constant expeditions beyond its borders.

www.ingramcontent.com/pod-product-compliance
Lightning Source LLC
Chambersburg PA
CBHW061936280526
45787CB00004B/1616